Pickups and Come-Ons

Lines for All Occasions

KNOCK KNOCK®

LOS ANGELES, CALIFORNIA

Created and published by Knock Knock
11111 Jefferson Blvd. #5167
Culver City, CA 90231
knockknockstuff.com

This book is a work of humor meant solely for entertainment purposes.
Actually utilizing the lines contained herein may be illegal or lead to
bodily injury. The publisher and anyone associated with the production
of this book do not advocate breaking the law. In no event will Knock
Knock be liable to any reader for any damages, including direct, indi-
rect, incidental, special, consequential, or punitive arising out of or in
connection with the use of the lines contained in this book. So there.

ISBN: 978-1-68349-260-3
UPC: 825703-50124-7

20 19 18 17 16 15 14 13 12 11 10 9 8 7 6 5 4 3 2 1

Contents

Intro
Preparing to Make Your Move

Paralyzed by a fear of rejection? Unable to muster the courage to walk across a room and introduce yourself? Don't worry—it's not you, it's your words. More precisely, it's the words you lack. With the right lines, however, you'll find yourself emboldened to go where you've always dreamed of going: straight up to the object of your desire.

Singles are everywhere—to be precise, 111 million single people live in the United States, or about 45 percent of the adult population. But that doesn't mean it's easy to find a date. Witness the explosion of dating sites and apps in recent years: today, 35 million Americans participate in online dating. Nevertheless, the majority of couples still meet offline—through friends, at bars, work, school, etc.—according to research by sociologists from Stanford University and the University of New Mexico. Simply put, meeting people IRL tends to yield the best results, says marriage and family therapist Amie Harwick: "When meeting someone in real life, you have the benefit of eye contact, viewing nonverbal cues, and judging a connection."

In other words, to succeed at dating in the digital age you still need a well-stocked arsenal of real-time pickup lines and come-ons, not merely thumb-typed bons mots.

Given the number of singles, the dating pool is not lacking warm bodies, and it's a well-known fact that everyone is looking for love—or at least a hookup. One can only assume, therefore, that people lack the words—and thus the courage—to make the first move. As *The Atlantic* put it in a 2019 article entitled "Why It's So Hard for Young People to Date Offline," we live in a time when "social-media skills are often conflated with social skills, and when the simple question of what to say out loud to another person can be anxiety-inducing for many."

Fortunately, *Pickups and Come-Ons for All Occasions* gives you the tools to cruise. Whether you study in advance or carry this pocket-sized volume for reference, you'll never again be at a loss for lines. Life is increasingly complex and demanding, and few of us have time to come up with our own powerful pickups, so we've done the work for you.

As you learn to use these lines, you'll no doubt face some rejection. Fear not! The law of averages is in your favor. If at first a line doesn't succeed, try, try again. One of these lines—somewhere, sometime—will prevail. Positive thoughts create positive outcomes, while stinkin' thinkin' does just the opposite. Having *Pickups and Come-Ons* in your pocket or purse will not only prepare you for any romance-seeking situation, it will give you the confidence to conduct yourself enthusiastically in any kind of introductory endeavor.

All About You

WHEN FLATTERY WILL GET YOU EVERYWHERE

"WOW, YOU LOOK GREAT!"

Doesn't that feel good? Exactly! Such is the simple art of the compliment. With a little more thought and wit—and a lot more of this book—you'll be turning the compliment into a pickup device in no time.

Focusing on others is one of the surest ways to win their attention and interest. Start slowly, flattering someone's overall appearance. Or you can focus on specific features: "great eyes" or "nice smile." Even complimenting a hottie's jacket, purse, or dress will send a clear message if you deliver it with appropriate feeling. The goal is to make your targets feel good about themselves, so good that they'll be willing to talk to you—or more.

Other approaches include corny compliments—saccharine-sweet sentiments sure to make the object of your attraction laugh and, hopefully, melt into your arms. Use sparingly and with humor to avoid the adverse gag-and-flee response. If charm isn't your thing, however, you could try the more risky teasing technique. Although it

Spread
Some
Sugar

sounds counterintuitive, some pickup artists believe a slightly insulting strategy works.

So take the first step: one little compliment, or perhaps a daring little dig, could go a long way. As a beginning romancer, you haven't much to lose.

Sometimes complimenting strangers really pays off. The You Are Beautiful project started in Chicago in 2002 when its creator, Matthew Hoffman, printed 200 "You Are Beautiful" stickers and posted them around town. The response inspired Hoffman to expand: "There were letters about how people came across a sticker and wanted their own to create these moments for others." Since then, the business has grown into a global enterprise involving thousands of artists, hundreds of art installations, and millions of stickers, stamps, and T-shirts bearing one simple message.

SKIN DEEP

Is it a burden being
that beautiful?

~

You should
be a model.
Seriously.

~

May I worship you
from a-near?

~

Have you always
been this cute,
or did you have
to practice?

~

Clearly all the
other women are
just rough drafts—
because you're
the final copy.

Someone call
Isaac Newton—
you're defying the
laws of gravity.

~

Is your name
Adonis?

~

Is that an
angel on your
shoulder, or am I
seeing double?

~

Nice to meet you.
I'm Cindy, and you
are . . . gorgeous.

~

When God made
you, she was
showing off.

What does it feel like to be the most attractive person in this room?

Did the sun come out, or did you just smile at me?

~

If beauty were time, you'd be eternity.

Michelangelo couldn't have carved anything more beautiful than you.

It's a felony in this state to look that good, but if you go out with me, I'll let you off with a warning.

I'd use a line on you, but I'm too intimidated by your beauty.

If you could put a price tag on beauty, you'd need to be driven around in an armored truck.

If I had a nickel for every time I saw someone as beautiful as you, I'd have five cents.

Something's wrong with my eyes—I can't take them off you.

Your father must have been a mailman, because you've got a great package.

HUBBA HUBBA

Apart from being sexy, what do you do for a living?

Just where exactly do those legs of yours end?

Damn, girl, you have more curves than a racetrack.

Do you have a license for those guns?

Damn, boy, is that a twelve-pack?

Good News for Average Joes

Baby, I've got the fries to go with that shake.

Your father must have been a mechanic, because your body is finely tuned.

If it weren't for that damn sun, you'd be the hottest thing ever created.

Someone better get a firehose quick 'cause you're smokin'.

As hot as you are, you must be contributing to global warming.

I want to wash my laundry on your abs.

I must have a light switch on my forehead, because you turn me on.

Don't hesitate to pick up on beautiful women if you lack in looks. Hotties do go out with notties, thanks in part to genetic percentages. There are simply more stunning women than men. A study in the *Journal of Theoretical Biology* submits that attractive parents are 36 percent more likely to give birth to girls, statistically increasing the number of beautiful women. So step up to the plate, guys—the babes may not be out of your league.

CORN SYRUP

I'm sorry to tell you that you're going to hell, because it's a sin to look that good.

    &

Your license ought to be suspended cause you're totally driving me crazy, baby.

    &

If I were a pirate, you would be my booty.

    &

Stop, drop, and roll, baby— you are on *fire*.

    &

You make me want to get a job.

You're like a dictionary—you add meaning to my life.

    &

If I could rearrange the alphabet, I'd put U and I together.

    &

Come live in my heart and pay no rent.

    &

Are you from Tennessee? Because you're the only ten I see.

    &

Will you plant a garden with me?

How was heaven
when you left it?

~

See these keys? I
wish I had the one
to your heart.

~

Quick, somebody
call the cops—
you just stole
my heart.

~

I never had a
dream come true
until today.

~

I hope you have
a map, because I
keep getting lost
in your eyes.

You must be
tired, because
you've been
running through
my mind all day.

~

I'm an artist,
and I think I just
found my muse.

~

You just made
being an artist
harder, because I
will never create
something as
beautiful as you.

~

I hope you
know CPR,
because you take
my breath away.

How did you guess? Sweetness is my weakness.

If we ever broke up, you'd be the one that got away.

Your eyes are bluer than the ocean, and baby, I'm lost at sea.

I've never seen someone as attractive as you who wasn't on film.

I don't know you, but I think I love you.

Everyone's got their thing. In our case, that thing would be perfection.

You look like the type of woman who's heard every line in the book, so what's one more?

Nice Guys Finish First

Way to go, God!

Didn't we meet in one of my dreams last week?

I'd pretend to go do volunteer work if you went out with me.

Can I be the last person on Earth that you go out with?

If we were in a movie right now, I'd be John Cusack outside your window holding up a radio.

Good thing my phone has GPS, because I'm lost in your eyes.

I'd buy you a drink but I'd get jealous of the glass.

Harvard researchers have proven that being nice works. When playing the theoretical game Prisoner's Dilemma, subjects who cooperated with one another ended up with the most money. Additionally, Harvard psychologist Elizabeth S. Spelke notes that people most prefer to share with three groups of people: close relations; those who have shared with us; and those who have shared with others. As *Scientific American* puts it, "We like to reward generosity even if it is not directed at us."

Can I take you off
the market?

Do you mind
if I end this
sentence in a
proposition?

I could fall
madly in bed
with you.

I'm very
articulate when
you're not around.

You can stop
looking. You've
found me.

You can't expect
me to believe
you don't have
a fan club.

Are you an alien?
Because you just
abducted my heart.

I should get a second
career as your stunt
double, because
I'm obviously
falling for you.

Speak
Fluent
Body
Language

If we were on *The Bachelor*, I'd give you the final rose.

Swans turn to you for lessons in grace.

I bet our kids will be beautiful with your eyes.

Your juiciness makes peaches jealous.

If you were any hotter, you'd come with a warning label.

If they filmed our story, it would be the perfect balance of rom and com.

Experts say body language communicates more than half of your message, so be aware! Skillful body language can subconsciously suggest compatibility to your target. Take your hands out of your pockets. Synchronize your movements with hers. Place an item in her personal space. Lean back when you converse to indicate power and confidence. Keep your hands still, not fidgety. Or, if you're not into subtle, you can always ask politely for a quick first kiss.

All About Me

WHEN YOU'RE OBVIOUSLY GOD'S GIFT

A BIG EGO MEANS A LOT OF CONFIDENCE, and confidence is a very seductive trait. With these lines, you can communicate that self-assurance to your target. Whether you're honestly assessing your assets or exaggerating them for effect, others will respect your poise and certainty. People are attracted to a healthy dose of self-love, so go ahead and brag.

To best harness this technique, get into the mindset before unleashing your pickup line. You are the greatest, and meeting you will make someone's day. Whether you're flaunting your good looks, bank account, or sexual prowess, by publicizing your strengths you will be giving your intended a little taste of what's in store.

Determine your approach to maximize your endowments and minimize your shortcomings. If your looks fall a little short, deflect attention to your bedroom skills or your big fat wallet. If you're broke, make note of your artistic integrity or smooth moves.

If all else fails, try another direction—woe is you. Capitalize on your misfortune and

Wind
Beneath
My
Wing

embody the opposite of the big ego by telling your sad, sad tale. Let sympathy and pity do the heavy lifting. If you under-score stories of your pathetic life with lost-puppy-dog eyes, who will be able to resist?

Above all, open and close with the biggest self-confidence booster around, positive think-ing: assume you are desired and it will be so.

A wingman is a time-honored trick for dudes on the prowl. A lesser-known twist is the *wingwoman*: a gal pal recruited to help break the ice with females. It's said, though, that for heterosexual men, the ideal wingman is gay. "A gay man can help inject a bit of humour into things—we can be a little cheekier than you," writes col-umnist Justin Myers in British *GQ*. A gay friend will also make a straight guy look more evolved—always a plus!

COCKY AF

As a matter of fact, I *am* God's gift to women!

~

Did you hear the latest health report? You need to up your intake of Vitamin Me.

~

Congratulations! We just held a secret lottery, and the grand prize is a night with me.

~

My name is Doug. That's "God" spelled backward, with a little bit of *U* in it.

My name is Justin . . . just incredible.

~

When God was creating Earth, he said, "Let there be perfection," and then there was me.

~

Do you have a name, or can I call you mine?

~

If somebody were to write your biography, the climax would be meeting me.

~

First buy me a drink, and then we'll talk.

People are in your life for a reason, a season, or a lifetime, and baby, when it comes to me, two out of three ain't bad.

ค

Not many guys are special enough to get me to talk to them.

ค

You already have a *boy*friend? Well, when you want a *man*friend, come see me.

ค

You just may be good enough to bear my children.

I can't wait for the day your laugh starts to annoy me.

ค

This is your lucky day—I just happen to be single.

ค

Okay, I'm here! What's your second wish?

ค

Hi, I'm Mr. Right. Someone said you were looking for me.

ค

Real men don't need pickup lines.

ALL ABOUT ME

I'M TOO SEXY

Damn! And I thought *I* was good-looking!

You know, I need a license to carry these guns.

I know it's dark, but trust me, I'm the hottest one here.

Why don't you drop the zero and get with a hero?

Fortunately for you, I'm more than just eye candy.

Are you really as beautiful as you seem, or do you just remind me of myself?

Must you stare?

They say a picture is worth a thousand words, but mine is insured for a million.

Simply Beastly

You know, when the light hits your eyes from this angle, I can see myself.

I thought I'd come over before you and your friends start fighting over me.

❧

❧

You're definitely a 9, but you'd be a perfect 10 if you were with me.

You seem to have the confidence to be with someone as good-looking as me.

❧

❧

Don't hate me because I'm beautiful. Instead, love me because I'll reflect well on you.

Do you believe in love at first sight, or should I walk by again?

For singles, Valentine's Day may not be the happiest of holidays, but at least we're not living in ancient Rome. The holiday traces its origin back to the feast of Lupercalia, a three-day festival where single men would beat single women with the skins of sacrificed dogs and goats, a practice believed to promote fertility. Couples were partnered by lottery—and apparently were expected to fornicate for the length of the festival.

ALL ABOUT ME

HELLA RICH

Have you ever
made love on a
pile of money?

Someone as
beautiful as you
deserves someone
as rich as me.

My chef makes
the best breakfast
you've ever tasted.

Your eyes are the
exact same color
as my Bentley.

I'm rich, you're
hot. What more
do we need?

Have you ever made
out in the back
seat of a Ferrari?

Do you have change
for a ten-thousand-
dollar bill?

Come for a swim
in my bathtub.

I hate to use another
lame pickup line,
but who needs class
when you got cash?

My yacht's only
forty feet long,
but I've got a hell
of a personality.

Do you want my phone number, or would you just like to google it?

I want a man who can see past my obscene wealth to the *real* me.

If it doesn't work out between us, you'll walk away with the summerhouse and half of my assets.

Let's blow this joint and make love in one of my five mansions.

I don't look like much, but wait until you see my bank account.

I can't wait to come home and find you sitting in my favorite 1680 Louis XV armchair.

Does money run in your family? Well, it does in mine.

My money can't make me happy, but you can.

You know, I'm actually not that tall. I'm just sitting on my wallet.

I can't take you to heaven, but my private helicopter can get you close.

I GOT MOVES

I can last all night without a plug or batteries.

I love bananas.

I may not be religious, but I do speak in tongues.

How would you like never to have to fake it again?

I'm not Fred Flintstone, but I'll make your bed rock.

You know how they say skin is the largest organ? Not in my case.

Tip: The Subtle Boast

Don't you recognize me from your wildest dreams?

When they tested Viagra, I was the control group.

It's not the size of the boat, it's the motion in the ocean.

I'm not a yes man. More of a "yes, yes, YES" man.

You don't know me, but you've been shouting my name for years.

Forget pillow talk. Let's go for pillow scream.

Some pickup targets will be put off by overt crowing, so you'll want to learn some tricks to imply your assets without coming off as a total peacock. The restrained approach requires a deft, roundabout touch. Rather than saying you went to Yale, reminisce about a favorite New Haven haunt. Offhandedly mention that you need a receipt for your manager or broker. Talk about the quality of the light in Paris. The stealthy impression will be priceless.

WOE IS ME

Bring a fire
hose 'cause I'm
smokin' in bed.

∽

I took a class at the
Learning Annex.

∽

I come with
references.

∽

I grind so fine, they
call me coffee.

∽

Hey, just watch
how I dance.

∽

I can do the splits—
both ways.

The great thing
about being so
average and
unappealing is that
I overcompensate
in other ways.

∽

My ex emptied our
bank account and
ditched me and the
kids to move to the
Bahamas. With
my best friend.
And our dog.

Cultivating
the Inner
Coach

I lost the lottery today. Please make me feel like a winner.

I just got dumped. Would you boost my self-esteem?

I've never NOT faked it. Wanna make an honest woman of me?

I have to turn myself in tomorrow, and I could get life.

I promised my therapist I would at least *try* to ask someone out.

A close relative died today, and I could really use the support.

Confidence is by far one of the most sexually attractive traits. The negative messages we replay in our heads have been scientifically shown to subliminally communicate to others and derail positive interactions, so you should go into every pickup situation reciting your own positive mantra (e.g., "I am the hottest person here tonight" or "I have stellar verbal skills"). Should you accidentally say it out loud, all the better.

Context-Specific

IF YOU'RE IN THE SAME PLACE, YOU'VE ALREADY got something in common—location, location, location! Drawing on shared interests, from love of sun and sand to contempt for laundry day, is one of the best ways to initiate an encounter and ensure subsequent meetings in new places of interest.

Don't let any opportunity for a pickup pass you by. Even the most mundane activities are laced with the chance to meet and greet. Whether standing in line for your morning coffee, photocopying office memos, or taking it to another level on the Stairmaster, look around—your dream date (or just tonight's date) could be right next to you. And if he or she is, you'll want to be prepared with the right words.

Every location can inspire its own made-to-order lines simply by incorporating the vocabulary of the setting, offering to help with the place-specific activity, or remarking on goings-on. This chapter provides come-ons for various environments, from the beach to the café, from the retirement home to the yoga class. After studying these lines, you'll be able to improvise at any locale by utilizing or adapting the accoutrements at hand.

Tip: Ignite the Spark.

Location-specific overtures go beyond the standard pickup and tip into the arena of small talk. When you make a clever, contextualized comment, it seems improvised and off-the-cuff rather than calculated or smarmy. And when you appear witty, natural, and spontaneous, you'll be a magnet for attraction!

If you lack sex appeal, don't fret. Just be sure to put yourself in exciting situations—especially on dates. According to the Schachter-Singer theory, any strenuous or thrilling situation produces the same symptoms as physical attraction (racing heart, sweaty palms, rapid breathing). So invite your date to ride a roller coaster, see a scary film, or take a hike. They may well think it's you getting them hot.

CONTEXT-SPECIFIC

BEACH

I think you
missed a spot.

I'd love to see you
in a Speedo.

❧

❧

You're the hottest
thing since sunburn.

Didn't I see you
coming out of
the ocean on a
giant seashell?

❧

Want to jump in
the ocean with
me? 'Cause you've
got me on fire.

❧

Come quick—
my sand castle
needs a queen!

❧

Can I borrow
your sunglasses?
Your beauty is
blinding me.

❧

Let's make crazy
tan lines together.

CAFÉ

❧

Excuse me—do
you happen to
like long walks
along the beach?

I like my coffee
like I like my men:
hot, tall, and strong.

Can I warm that up for you?

I get horny when I'm caffeinated.

With you around, I don't need sugar in my coffee.

Is this seat free? Because I am.

GROCERY STORE

Do you like it steamy? Creamy? Or both?

You better get out of that express lane, 'cause you're all that *and* a bag of chips.

I have to admit I'm a little jealous of your laptop.

I've got some meat here that's "best if used by tonight."

I can't finish my pastry. Would you like a bite?

It looks like I picked the right checkout line.

CONTEXT-SPECIFIC

GYM

From the looks of
your cart, and the
tone of your abs,
you must be on
the paleo diet.

You look like you
could kick some ass.

I've always wondered
what to do with
leeks. What do you
do with them?

My heart rate
always hits the
red zone when
you're around.

Can you tell
if these melons
are ripe?

It's nearly
impossible to make
bike shorts look
good—but you do.

Can you help me
find the honey?

The Most
Unlikely
Places

How 'bout them
apples?

I could use an extra
workout tonight.

I can tell
you've got great
stamina.

When God
invented Lycra,
he was thinking
about you.

Would you
spot me?

LAUNDRO-MAT

You know, there's
another way to
do high-intensity
intervals.

Is this thong
yours? I found it
in the dryer.

According to the *Los Angeles Times*, Stan Rosenfield
was in the hospital, about to undergo a colonoscopy,
when he noticed an anxious, attractive woman on the
gurney next to his. He chatted her up and learned that
she was nervous about having the same procedure.
After reassuring her, he got her phone number and later
took her to dinner. The moral of the story? No place (and
no outfit—hospital gowns?) is off-limits for a pickup.

The whites go
in with the red
socks, right?

~

Does that stain
have a story?

~

It's the spin cycle—
my favorite.

~

So . . . you bleach?

~

Oh, no, I forgot
detergent!

~

Let's make our
clothes dirty all
over again.

You must use
a ton of fabric
softener, because
your skin looks as
smooth as silk.

CANNABIS DISPENSARY

Just looking at
you gives me a
contact high.

~

There's nothing
here I'd rather wrap
my lips around and
smoke than you.

~

Whoa. That's
the same ultra-
potent strain I was
going to pick!

You're my new
favorite edible.

WWJD? Tell you
to go out with me.

~

You are totally
blazing.

I had a revelation
about you.

~

I could get
addicted to you.

Could we pray
together sometime?

~

Let's make like
love muffins and
get totally baked.

With those muscles,
you could lug any
size Torah around.

~

PLACE OF WORSHIP

Seriously, you're
beautiful, but
it's your soul I'm
interested in.

Is it a sin that you
stole my heart?

~

I predicted David
over Goliath.

CONTEXT-SPECIFIC

YOGA

Is that a crystal
wand in your pocket,
or are you just
glad to see me?

I see that
you're bendy.

❧

❧

I met Sting once.

God gave us these
urges. Who are we
to deny them?

❧

How would you like
a sneak preview
of Nirvana?

Do you need
help with your
inversion?

❧

God, how do
you do that?

❧

You're going to
send me right
to confession.

Come-On
Contract

❧

You know Jesus?
Hey, me too!

I sure do
like your
downward dog.

Let's practice our
breathwork together.

NURSING HOME

It's a shame
you don't walk
around in leotards
all day long.

Have you ever
made love on a
motorized scooter?

Before coming
to this class,
I specialized
in tantric.

I didn't know
parts of me still
worked until
I saw you.

Thinking about picking up someone at work? You
may first want to sign the flirting version of a prenup,
the "consensual relationship agreement," AKA the love
contract. Originated by the prominent employment
law firm Littler Mendelson, the document, signed by
coworkers about to embark on an affair, proclaims that
both parties are entering into the relationship consensu-
ally, protecting everybody involved from future harass-
ment charges.

CONTEXT-SPECIFIC

If it weren't for
my trick knee, I'd
sweep you right
off your feet.

You make me feel
seventy again.

SCHOOL

I'm glad I
have a library
card because
I really like
checking you out.

I've got prescriptions
that'll blow
your mind.

You'd be amazed
what I can do
without my dentures.

You're by far my
favorite subject.

You make the
feeling come back
in my legs.

My memory isn't
what it used to be.
Have we met before?

Wanna get together and cram?

I'm majoring in English and I still can't describe your beauty.

I'm minoring in *Kama Sutra* studies.

You may not be that smart, but your body's an A-plus.

The teacher thought I was cheating because I can't take my eyes off you.

Your dorm room or mine?

When you're out looking for Mr. or Ms. Right Now, be prepared. The Centers for Disease Control estimates that 20 million new STD infections occur each year. Carry unexpired condoms and be prepared to prove your HIV status. While healthy protocols and disease-free status will help you once you've attracted a potential partner, avoid incorporating them into your pickups; "Hey, baby, the clinic says I'm clean now" is generally not a winner.

CONTEXT-SPECIFIC

People-Specific

COMPLEMENTARY TO THE PLACE-SPECIFIC pickup line is the person- or role-specific come-on. You might not know his name, but you know what he does—and he does it well. Referencing someone's livelihood is a classic approach and a great icebreaker. Whether your interaction is a one-time occurrence or you see someone on a day-to-day basis, talking with your target about her profession and skills will open the door.

As with location-specific pickups, these lines earn points for focus and creativity. You can pick up on career-related interests and play to your crush's expertise. Most likely he already knows a little—or a lot—about you, too: what you like to drink, how much you tip, where you live, or, in the case of a therapist, your deep inner thoughts. This can generate appeal or aversion, so play your cards carefully.

In addition to peppering your come-ons with vocational lingo, you'll want to consider unique approaches to suit individual professions. A hot bartender probably hears a lot of lines, so make yours intriguing. For a customer service rep, use a sultry tone for delivery. A doctor has seen it all, so add a little mystery. And for the therapist, go for the breakthrough.

Effective Flirting

Your goal, of course, is to make your way into a hardworking person's heart via their chosen livelihood. Best of all, unlike with many pickups, you can be sure in these instances that your future paramour is employed.

By practicing a few easy techniques, you'll be able to attract all types of hotties. First, when he's talking, listen and pay attention; don't be thinking of what *you* are going to say next. Then, mimic and rephrase: mirror his body language and verbal style, restating and agreeing with his comments. Repeat his name whenever possible. Finally, ask questions: make him feel like the center of your universe. The most important tip? Smile.

BARTENDER	PHONE REP
What time do you get off, and how?	Ooh, does that accent mean you're in India?
↬	↬
If you get any closer, I'll need more ice.	No, thank you for *taking* my call.
↬	↬
I've got great problems. Do you want to hear about them?	I bet you look really sexy in a headset.
↬	↬
I like it shaken, not stirred, because you shake so well.	Have you considered doing voice-over work?
↬	↬
You're strictly top-shelf.	I can't imagine you process returns for just anybody.

DOCTOR

I'd drop my pants for you any day.

I'm an organ donor— need anything?

*

You really raise my blood pressure.

You palpate so gently.

*

I feel like you can really see inside me, and it's not just the X-rays.

With a bedside manner like that, I can't imagine how anybody ever lets you out of bed.

*

Would you prefer my gown open in the front or back?

GARDENER

Let's give "mow, blow, and go" a whole new meaning.

*

I'm not afraid of needles, but I prefer being otherwise penetrated.

Would you like another hedge to trim?

GEEK

Other men may bring me flowers, but you tend them.

You're so good with my software. I can really help with your hardware.

~

~

Is it hard to handle a hose that big?

I wear *Mortal Kombat* cosplay on weekends.

~

So what made you decide to specialize in the horticultural field?

~

What's a maiden like you doing in a dungeon like this?

~

When I think of what your hands do to my plants, I can only imagine what they could do to me.

~

I wouldn't mind being fertilized.

Your graphics rival *Star Wars Battlefront II*.

I hope you don't have a firewall, because I want to access all your ports.

You may be a geek by day, but I bet you're a sex machine by night!

I'll input if you'll output.

I'd be proud to attend Comic-Con with you.

BLUE-COLLAR WORKER

My hinge could use a little grease.

When trying to determine whether someone is interested, look for these signals. Does she square off to face you? Look at your mouth a lot? Preen or adjust clothing, jewelry, or hair? Have raised eyebrows? Expose palms or wrists to you? Lean toward you when you speak? Have dilated pupils? Touch you during conversation? If you're lucky enough to catch a few of these physical clues, know that you're on the right track, headed for the station.

COURIER

I feel so close to
you now that you've
plunged my toilet.

Wow, that's quite
a package.

That tool belt really
brings out the green
in your eyes.

I could think of
something *else*
I'd like from
you instead.

Would you like
to nail me?

I see where to sign
my name, but
where can I leave
my number?

Can you hammer
all day long?

This box may have
been sent by
ground, but you're
strictly overnight.

My, you're handy.

What a big,
beautiful toolbox.

Wow, you sure
do deliver.

They didn't mention I'd get such special handling.

You've got sirens, I *am* a siren— it's perfect!

You already know where I live. Do you have any other questions?

What do you do with those handcuffs when you're not working?

POLICE OFFICER

I bet you're a top-notch shooter.

You didn't just pull me over for a citation, right?

Want to run me through your system?

I love a man in a uniform— but I like it even better when he's out of his uniform.

My driver's license doesn't do my nude pictures justice.

FIREFIGHTER

Haven't I seen you on a calendar?

Is it safe for a firefighter to be so totally smokin'?

I'd love to slide down your pole.

Please help me put out this bushfire.

I bet you're good at unscrewing tight hydrants.

STORE CLERK

Was "Leave a penny, take a penny" your idea?

Would you show me how you unroll your hose?

Can you show me the correct way to perform mouth-to-mouth?

Nice Package

Can you recommend a good malt liquor?

Let's do something for the hidden camera!

Did you major in retail services?

If I were to shoplift, what would you do to me?

I'd love to have you check me out.

THERAPIST

I love to watch you fill my bag.

Enough about me— what is it that relaxes *you*?

People love receiving parcels, especially from an attractive delivery person. According to the *Wall St. Journal*, UPS couriers have inspired "brown-collar fantasies" for decades. But when FedEx ramped up its ground game in 2000, a "whose uniform is sexier?" rivalry arose between couriers. Both services have resulted in countless dates and even some marriages. Still, with its 1-800-PICK-UPS number, UPS remains a thirsty fave.

PEOPLE-SPECIFIC

I think I could have
a breakthrough
if you sat on the
couch with me.

Pretty sure I'd
benefit from some
sexual healing. What
do you advise?

SERVER

How do I
really feel? Soft
and silky.

The menu
looks good.
Are you on it?

You remind
me of my first
memory of sex.

Oh, I like it hot.
Hot and spicy.

How can you
truly know me
without coming
over to my house
for drinks?

Sexy Quotes

One word—oedipal.

It's only fair: you're serving me dinner, I'll cook you breakfast.

Is there anything that's *not* on the menu?

I'd like to try something exotic. What do you recommend?

I'll have the cheese balls.

Don't you have any *other* condiments?

I'm a vegetarian, but you make me wanna eat meat.

"A rainbow of color strikes the eyelids. A foam of music falls over the ears. It is the gong of the orgasm." —Anaïs Nin

"Sexual intercourse is kicking death in the ass while singing." —Charles Bukowski

"In my sex fantasy, nobody ever loves me for my mind." —Nora Ephron

"Making eye contact during rough sex is roughly the equivalent of trying to read Dostoyevsky on a roller coaster." —Jenna Jameson

"I used to be Snow White . . . but I drifted." —Mae West

PEOPLE-SPECIFIC

Rela-tionships

WHEN YOU'RE
PLAYING FOR KEEPS

LET'S BE HONEST—A PICKUP OR A COME-ON is, at its most basic, an invitation for sex.

The delight (or difficulty) of joining a committed relationship is that this pursuit never ends, even after you've sworn lifelong fidelity. That's right, folks: if you want a successful long-term relationship, you have to court one another—lest you end up in court.

The goal of commitment is not merely a lack of cheating. The goal of stability is not a lackluster substitute for the thrill of the chase. The goal of a long-term romance is sustained—and even full-blown—desire for one another. It's eternal longing—even as you muddle through the minefields of parenting and middle age. Even as your bodies weaken and your short-term memory banks go bust.

Is such a thing even possible? Of course it is—and it's good for you. According to expert Howard S. Friedman Ph.D., coauthor of The Longevity Project, "A sexually satisfying and happy marriage is a very good predictor of future health and long life." We still don't fully understand why and how marriage and sex make us live longer (and happier) but we

Pop the Question(s)

know that they do. (Even unmarried committed couples live longer than singles.)

Whether you want to park the pink Cadillac, make the beast with two backs, or bump uglies, sex is what it's all about. A full arsenal of come-ons will serve you and your partner well over the years. You can start with the lines in this chapter. From the suggestive to the scandalous to the simply silly, these lines are built to last—hopefully, just like your sex life.

～

What becomes a couple most? According to four Harvard mathematicians (who cofounded OG dating service OK Cupid), if you and your date agree on the answers to the following questions, you stand a far greater chance of becoming a couple.

- Do you like horror movies?
- Have you ever traveled around another country alone?
- Wouldn't it be fun to chuck it all and go live on a sailboat?

SHACKING UP

Even when you have
morning breath,
you're the first thing
I want to smell
every morning.

~

I'm really good at
playing house.

~

Wanna mingle
our undies?

~

I want a lifetime
of your morning
bedhead.

~

If we were peasants,
I'd always sleep
on the drafty side
of the hay pile.

We can get rid of all
my weird furniture.

~

I love you so much
I don't care that
you take up nine-
tenths of the bed
every night.

~

Would you fill my
bathroom with
your products?

~

Would you come
take up more than
your fair share of
closet space?

~

We're gonna need
a bigger bed.

I love you even though I smash my knee when I get in the car because you never move the seat back.

I didn't just fall in love with you, it was a complete face plant.

KISSING UP

My lips never get tired of kissing you.

With a wife like you, every night is like date night.

~

~

All your sweet nothings mean something to me.

You really are my partner in crime, because you always steal my heart.

~

~

I could get used to all these fireworks.

Are you a race car driver? Because you went from sweetheart to spouse in no time.

~

Do you get tired of being right all the time?

Why go out?
Everyone I
need is here.

A day without you
is like forgetting
to take out the
garbage—it
just stinks.

Those pants look
perfect on you.

I was just stuffing
large gherkins in a
tight pickle jar and
thought of you.

DAILY LIFE:
KITCHEN

How about tonight
I can do the dishes,
and you can do me?

Let's skip dinner and
get right to dessert.

You can drink milk
straight from the
carton anytime.

I'll give you another
reason to clear the
table right now.

You can have the last bite of pie.

Can we fight over dinner so we can have make-up sex for dessert?

I'm thinking of toasting some buns—bring those over here.

In my kitchen, melons are always ripe.

This jar lid is screwed on so tight—can you open it for me?

The sink isn't the only thing that's wet in this kitchen.

Science may have found a cure for the unfaithful lover, thanks to our tiny rodent friend the vole. It seems one type of vole is monogamous, while another is a rampant philanderer. But when researchers injected the cheater voles with a neurochemical combo of oxytocin and vasopressin, the furry little cads abandoned their debauched ways and stuck with their longterm mates. So . . . if monogamy is just an injection away, will health insurance cover it?

I'd eat kale for you.

Wanna share
my Nutella?

I've got a sizzling
loin I'd like
you to taste.

The fact that you
wash and reuse
sandwich bags is
cute, not gross.

DAILY LIFE:
BATHROOM

I'm no artist, but
I'd love to draw
you a bath.

You had me at "I'll
clean the bathroom."

How about I give
you a facial?

Baby, I'll clean your
drain any day.

I don't even mind
if you use my
toothbrush.

DAILY LIFE:
LAUNDRY

Laundry's not
the only thing
that's going for
a spin in here.

PARENTING

Only you can
make washing
clothes look sexy.

Accidentally
knocking you
up was the best
thing that ever
happened to me.

That pillow isn't the
only thing that needs
fluffing around here.

I say if we don't
wake at least
one kid in this
house, we're not
doing it right.

They call it a
dryer, but it tends
to get me wet.

You're the
hottest MILF at
the playground.

Maybe we should
test that new stain
remover I bought.

I can't rip
those dad
jeans off you
fast enough.

You have anything
you want to take
off and throw in
with this load?

The kids are
asleep . . .

Your fertility-
goddess body
makes me hot.

I installed a lock on
our bedroom door.

You make
minivans sexy.

Wanna make
another one?

You're my own
personal DILF.

Even after saying
"I do," you still make
me want to do it.

You're always the
#1 item on my
"Honey-Do" list.

It's not too
late to follow our
dreams and start
training for the
Sex Olympics.

This Is
Your
Brain on
Love

Who needs
central heat when
you're around?

Sleeping with
you makes me
want to go to
the gym.

I'll warm
up your side
of the bed
any night.

You must be
an electrician,
because you sure
know how to keep
that spark alive.

Why would I
need porn when
I have you?

Can I help you
master your O face?

If the mere sight of the one you love gives you sweats
and causes your pulse to quicken, you have the ventral
tegmental area of your brain to thank. This tiny crumb of
gray matter is responsible for releasing both the stress
hormone norepinephrine as well as the pleasure-induc-
ing neurotransmitter dopamine—making love's potent
effect on the body approaching something close to that
of meth. Crazy in love, indeed!

You know
what I like about
you? My arms.

I'm wearing a
matching bra
and panties.

You make
me ache in all the
right places.

I want you more
today than the first
time we had sex
in that nightclub
bathroom.

Let's get freaky
and freak out
the neighbors.

When you whisper
like that, I still
get chills.

If we just
met, I'd still
want to have a
one-night stand.

**Movies,
Between
Your
Legs**

Hearing your jeans
unzip still makes
my stomach jump.

I convinced my
mother to stay
in a hotel.

We can do that
as much as you
desire—or until my
other hip gives out.

GROWING OLDER

When I can't
remember my own
name, I'll still be
moaning yours.

I can do without
oxygen when
you're with me.

Your ears still taste
like peaches.

Believe me,
you'll clap every
night I take my
dentures out.

Next time you're Netflixing with your honey, have
some off-the-script fun with this game: take any
movie title and add "between my legs" for a marquee-
worthy tagline. As with appending the words "in bed"
to fortune-cookie fortunes ("You will soon achieve
success . . . in bed!"), this trick is a guaranteed rib-tick-
ler. "It's *Frozen* . . . between my legs!" "*A Star Is
Born* . . . between my legs!" The opportunities—and
fun—are endless.

Famous Flirtations

HAVE YOU EVER IMAGINED HOW GREAT YOUR pickup lines could be if they were written by Hollywood screenwriters, literary giants, television scribes, or rock stars? To provide you with come-on inspiration, this chapter presents a panoply of some of the best-loved and most clever pickup lines ever crafted.

The functionality of these lines doesn't end at inspiration—you can actually use them. You could choose to go the safe route (citing your source then discussing its provenance, i.e., where you were when you saw the movie, read the book, heard the song). Depending on the line, it could make you sound literate, intelligent, and cultured, or you could come off as a pop-culture junkie. If you feel you can get away with it, you could also try taking credit for the line as your own, sounding as smooth and as suave as the original creators did.

Pickups and come-ons have been around since the beginning of time—otherwise, how would the population have replaced itself? While many of the best no doubt went unrecorded (how many times do you stop to write down your best material?), there have been literary and musical types who've taken the time to

craft verbal moves—whether for themselves or for fictional characters—to perfection.

By now you're a pro at the pickup game. Once you're ready to go off-script, it'll be no surprise if your sweet-talking savvy makes its way into the next version of this book.

~

It turns out the next best thing to being in love is watching two people in a film do it . . . fall in love, that is. Neuropsychologist Dr. David Lewis says that when we see stars kiss onscreen, our brain's mirror neurons start firing. "Each person mistakenly attributes a part of the adrenaline buzz produced by the film to the presence of their partner." So the next time you watch a romantic movie like *The Notebook*, you'll know why you think the guy near you is Ryan Gosling.

FAMOUS FLIRTATIONS

FILM

"You know, when you blow out the match, it's an invitation to kiss you." —John Gilbert, *Flesh and the Devil*, 1926

"You're a swell dish. I think I'm gonna go for you." —James Cagney, *The Public Enemy*, 1931

"What's happenin', hot stuff?" —Gedde Watanabe, *Sixteen Candles*, 1984

"Swoon. I'll catch you." —Ralph Fiennes, *The English Patient*, 1996

"I don't know how to put this, but I'm kind of a big deal. People know me. I'm very important. I have many leather-bound books and my apartment smells of rich mahogany." —Will Ferrell, *Anchorman*, 2004

"Would you like to have dinner with us? It's just leftovers. Collard greens and corn bread, some candied yams, a little potato salad, fried chicken, peach cobbler, and a few slices of ham." —Loretta Devine, *Waiting to Exhale*, 1995

"Everything wrong with you, I like."
—Van Johnson, A *Guy Named Joe*, 1944

"We're going to know each other eventually, why not now?" —Humphrey Bogart, *Across the Pacific*, 1942

"I'd like to run barefoot through your hair."
—Franchot Tone, *Bombshell*, 1933

"I am looking for a 'dare to be great' situation."
—John Cusack, *Say Anything*, 1989

"You make me want to be a better man."
—Jack Nicholson, *As Good As It Gets*, 1997

"You know what's wrong with you? Nothing."
—Audrey Hepburn, *Charade*, 1963

"Can you keep a secret? I'm trying to organize a prison break. We have to first get out of this bar, then the hotel, then the city, and then the country. Are you in or you out?"
—Bill Murray, *Lost in Translation*, 2003

"I couldn't help but notice that you look a lot like my next girlfriend."—Will Smith, *Hitch*, 2005

"Have you ever done it in an elevator?" —Glenn Close, *Fatal Attraction*, 1987

"Was that cannon fire, or is it my heart pounding?" —Ingrid Bergman, *Casablanca*, 1942

"You're so beautiful, it makes me want to gag." —Jimmy Stewart, *You Can't Take It with You*, 1938

"Who am I? Well, they call me Brother to the night. And right now I'm the blues in your left thigh, trying to become the funk in your right. Is that all right?" —Larenz Tate, *Love Jones*, 1997

Classical Cussing

TELEVISION

"Why don't you come up sometime 'n' see me?" —Mae West, *She Done Him Wrong,* 1933

"I like your butt . . . I mean your bike." —Shannen Doherty, *90210,* 1990

~

~

"You know how they say we only use ten percent of our brains? I think we only use ten percent of our hearts." —Owen Wilson, *Wedding Crashers,* 2005

"How *you* doin'?" —Matt LeBlanc, *Friends,* 1994

~

"I'm a real good sex person." —Jack McBrayer, *30 Rock,* 2008

Naughty language in popular culture isn't new. A raunchy translation of Aristophanes' *Lysistrata* includes such slang as "ball," used as a verb, and Catullus was a big fan of a slur that rhymes with trick. In *The Canterbury Tales*, Chaucer used the cruder words for derriere, poop, piddle, and female anatomy (charmingly spelled with a "qu"). Shakespeare and Joyce had fun with tongue-in-cheek swearing like "See you in tea" and "If you see kay" (say them aloud).

"Maybe . . . this challenges what you thought you were. And . . . maybe I'm gonna get my heart broken in a thousand different pieces. But those are maybes. You can't live your life according to maybes." —Samira Wiley, *Orange Is the New Black*, 2016

"How about when the alert level goes down, and the terrorists have been caught, we can have some chamomile tea and I'll tell you all my secrets?" —Mary Lynn Rajskub, *24*, 2001

"I think I've seen your picture somewhere before. Oh yeah, that's right. It was in the dictionary next to KABLAM!" —Will Smith, *The Fresh Prince of Bel-Air*, 1995

"I figure a girl like you has heard all the phony lines in the book . . . so one more isn't going to hurt . . . Walk with me. Talk with me." —Andy Kaufman, *Taxi*, 1978

"Come and get me, sailors." —Kim Cattrall, *Sex and the City*, 2002

LITERATURE

"Graze on my lips; and if these hills be dry, / Stray lower, where the pleasant fountains lie." —William Shakespeare, "Venus and Adonis," 1593

ى

"License my roving hands, and let them go, / Before, behind, between, above, below." —John Donne, "To His Mistress Going to Bed," 1595

"See my lips tremble, and my eyeballs roll / Suck my last breath, and catch my flying soul." —Alexander Pope, "Eloisa to Abelard," 1717

ى

"I wrong you not if I my thoughts reveal, / Saying how the beauty that your clothes conceal / Is like a spark that sets afire my heart. / I only ask that you then, for your part, / Will be a saddle and let me ride, / Just for this once." — François Rabelais, *Gargantua and Pantagruel*, 1534

"Was this the face that launched a thousand ships, / And burnt the topless towers of Ilium? / Sweet Helen, make me immortal with a kiss!"
—Christopher Marlowe, *Doctor Faustus*, 1604

"But did thee feel the earth move?" — Ernest Hemingway, *For Whom the Bell Tolls*, 1940

MUSIC

"Hello, I love you / Won't you tell me your name? / Hello, I love you / Let me jump in your game."
—The Doors, "Hello I Love You," 1968

"O for you, whoever you are, your correlative body! O it, more than all else, you delighting!"
—Walt Whitman, *Leaves of Grass*, 1860

Producer vs. Receptors

"You're wet and you're warm just like our bathwater / Can we make love before you go?"
—Frank Ocean, "Pyramids," 2012

"Why do birds suddenly appear / Every time you are near? / Just like me, they long to be / Close to you."
—Burt Bacharach, "Close to You," 1963

"I wanna keep it how it is, so you can never say how it used to be." — Beyoncé, "Dance for You," 2011

"If you like piña coladas / And getting caught in the rain."
—Rupert Holmes, "Escape," 1979

It takes two to joke—the comic and the laugher, AKA the producer and the receptor. A sense of humor is desirable by both men and women. According to a university study, however, passive-active gender stereotypes prevail when joking around: women choose men who *produce* humor 62 percent of the time, while men choose women who *appreciate* their humor 65 percent of the time. At least it's even; let's hope the other 35 percent are LOL.

FAMOUS FLIRTATIONS

"If it took a war for us to meet it will have been worth it." —Lin-Manuel Miranda, "Satisfied," *Hamilton*, 2015

"There's a dazzling haze, a mysterious way about you, dear / Have I known you 20 seconds or 20 years?" —Taylor Swift, "Lover," 2019

"Give me little drink from your loving cup / Just one drink and I'll fall down drunk." —The Rolling Stones, "Loving Cup," 1972

"All the other girls here are stars—you are the Northern Lights." —Josh Ritter, "Kathleen," 2003

"When I'm taking sips from your tasty lips / Seems the honey fairly drips / Goodness knows / You're my honeysuckle rose." —Fats Waller, "Honeysuckle Rose," 1929

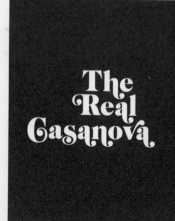

The Real Casanova

"All I want is one night of glory / I don't even know your second name." —Elvis Costello, "Different Finger," 1981

"I get no kick from champagne / Mere alcohol doesn't thrill me at all / So tell me why should it be true / That I get a kick out of you?" —Cole Porter, "I Get a Kick Out of You," 1934

"I'll take you to the candy shop / I'll let you lick the lollipop / Go 'head girl, don't you stop / Keep going 'til you hit the spot." —50 Cent, "Candy Shop," 2005

"Oooh, baby, baby / Baby, baby / Get up on this!" —Salt-N-Pepa, "Push It," 1987

The name synonymous with seduction, Casanova, is actually connected to a human being, eighteenth-century Venetian adventurer, intellect, author, and ladies' man Giovanni Giacomo Casanova. His autobiography, *Story of My Life*, details his numerous conquests (over one hundred!) with the fairer sex—and more. Orgies, threesomes, and voyeurism provide an authentic look at the not-so-old-fashioned European courting and mating customs of his age.